This book belongs to:

Ben

....

........Benjamin....Alafriz.........

Illustrations by Paula Knight (Advocate)
English language consultant: Betty Root

This is a Parragon Publishing book
First published in 2002

Parragon Publishing
Queen Street House
4 Queen Street
BATH, BA1 1HE, UK

ISBN   0-75257-767-0

Printed in China

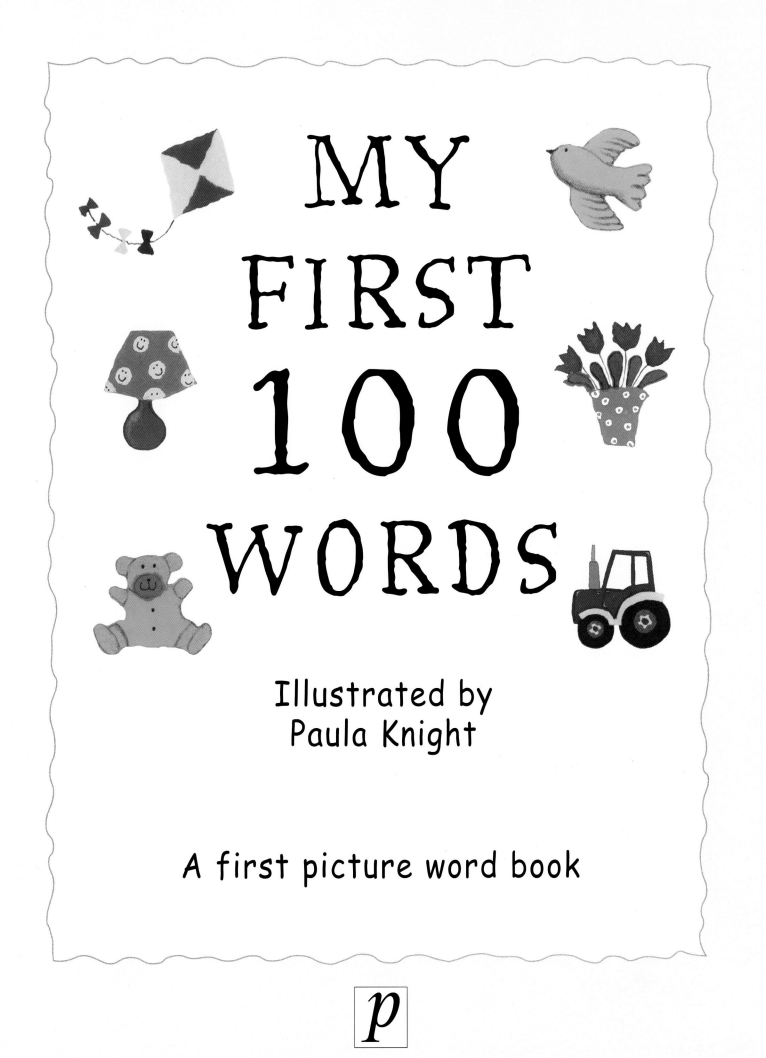

MY FIRST 100 WORDS

Illustrated by
Paula Knight

A first picture word book

p

My family

Mom   Dad   brother   sister

baby

Grandma

Grandpa

dog

In my home

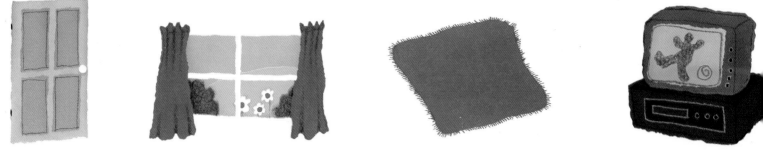

door   window   rug   television

chair   sofa   table   flowers

Getting dressed

undershirt   **underpants**   **shorts**   **pants**

skirt   socks   shoes   shirt   sweater

Mealtime

bowl

plate

pitcher

knife

fork  spoon  cup  saucer

Playtime

train   trumpet   drum   blocks

ack-in-the-box   doll   paints   puzzle

In the city

bus

truck

store

bicycle

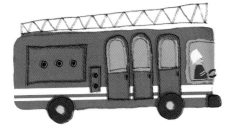

car   stroller   fire truck   motorcycle

In the park

swings   slide   seesaw   ball

gate   tree   bird   kite

At the beach

pail   shovel   ice cream   fish   sandcastle

t-shirt   crab   boat   shell

At the market

basket

cart

bananas

apples

orange

 carrots  bread  tomatoes  milk  cheese

On the farm

horse   cow   farmer   pig

 chicken

 cat

 sheep

 tractor

Bathtime

toothbrush

toothpaste

bathtub

duck   soap   towel   potty   sink

Bedtime

lamp

slippers

bed

cloc

 book

 moon

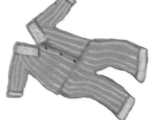 pajamas

 teddy bear